JN094921

I have lived

長応院墓地 親子地蔵尊

Parent and Child Jizo at Chohouin Buddhist Temple Cemetery

全

台東区立黒門小学校防空壕

Taito Ward Kuromon Elementary School Air Raid Shelter

空蓮房

Kurenboh Chohouin Buddhist Temple Gallery

I have lived a life

わたしは　生を　生きた

《ひと》2012年、空蓮房 | *human*, 2012, Kurenboh Chohouin Buddhist Temple Gallery

Human is a believer

Facing human human thinks human it is

Facing human human thinks hope it is

Facing hope human thinks human it is

Facing hope human thinks hope it is

そのひとはしんじるひと

ひとにむき　ひとともおもう

ひとにむき　きぼうともおもう

きぼうにむき　ひとともおもう

きぼうにむき　きぼうともおもう

見届けるということ

小池一子［東京ビエンナーレ 2020/2021 総合ディレクター］

「東京の地場に発するビエンナーレ」企画が生まれ、参画した私は台東区の小学校にある地下防空壕を展示サイトとして選んだ。戦争がいまだに止まない世界の中でかつてこの都市を襲った戦火を思うことが第一の動機である。「東京に祈る」という言葉が自然に口をついて出た。そしてそれを私の敬愛するアーティスト内藤礼さんに告げた。内藤さんがその言葉にすぐ応えてくれて、そこから心身が震えるような唯一無二の空間劇が始まった。

まず私のことから話そう。私は第二次世界大戦が日本列島に砲火の雨を降らせた時、“国民学校”（戦中の小学校の呼び名）の三年生だった。東京から義父母のいる静岡県の函南という山村に避難していた。これを個人疎開という。国は都会の子供をとにかく地方の親類、縁故先へ送れと命令していた。

義父は青年訓練所という名目のもとに日本が侵略した国々の青年を、寄宿生活を含めて農業と綿作に従事させる教習所の主宰者だった。静岡県の温暖な気候の中で、山草が茂り果実が熟す。小川のせせらぎの下には芹が青々と茂っていた。私は毎日のように川淵に座って足を流水に浸しながら同級生と童謡を歌っていた。軍歌ではなく。疎開した私は桃源郷の中にいたのだ。

山村にも防空壕は推奨され、山肌に小さな洞穴のような壕を義父が作った。東京を砲撃したB29機が使い残した爆弾を伊豆半島から沼津湾あたりに落としていくと大人の会話から知ったが、それは防空壕の中でのことであったかもしれない。戦時の日常に不意に敵機襲来という事態だから、防空壕の横穴の中では食事中に祖母としていた喧嘩を持ちこんで不愉快な時間を過ごしたことも思い出される。それでも私は家族と一緒だった。集団疎開で遠隔の見知らぬ土地に移動した子供たちはどんな思いを耐えていたのだろうか。

一方、都市の学校建築の中に集団の避難所としての防空壕を設置するという計画も進められていた。今回の東京ビエンナーレ2020/2021における内藤礼企画はその「校内に残された防空壕」を調査したことに始まっている。

敗戦とその後の復興についてはここで触れるまでもないが、防空壕はほとんど東京という都市の表面からは姿を消している。戦禍、災禍の記憶を風化させぬために、モニュメントを残すという行動も時間が経てば立ち消えていくのだ。だが東京ビエンナーレ事務局の丁寧な調査の結果、台東区の黒門小学校地下に戦時の空間が残されていることがわかった。

「東京に祈る」の命題は私たちを蔵前の寺院に併設された展示空間へと導く。長応院住職で写真家の谷口昌良さんの私設ギャラリーだ。建築家ヨコミゾマコトとの計画に添い設えられたミニマルで選ばれた外光が特徴的な空間だ。

内藤礼さんはそこに「ひと」を一人立たせる。

ひとは2011年、東日本大震災の後の沈黙の中から生まれた内藤さんの木製の形。最小の木の彫刻といってもいい。閉じられた空間に射す光の流れが、小さなひとのありかを見せる。

それから、長応院から1分ほど歩いた先に住職が私たちを連れて行く。普通の街の歩道に面した木戸を開けると、そこは墓地。一角に東京大空襲で命を奪われた子供たちのための慰霊の地蔵が立っている。内藤さんはお地蔵さんの前にガラスの瓶を置き、水を注ぐ。

水を求めてあの日、戦火の中で逃げ惑った人たちがいた、子供がいた。亡くなった女児男児の名前が地蔵の台石に刻まれている。その前に置くガラスの器はなんでもないびん、ガラス瓶の蓋をとった形である。殺された子供たちに差し出す水、東京ビエンナーレでこの会場を訪れた人たちが真夏の陽の下で蒸発する分を補っていくことになる。

内藤礼の展示は長応院のインスタレーションと墓地の祈りの背景を擁して、黒門小学校地下壕の空間構成で結実することになる。

現在は海外からの観光客で賑わう商店街からほど近い旧上野黒門町に建設されたこの公立小学校は1923年の関東大震災以降の耐震建築の代表的な例とも言える頑丈な作りで知られるが、地下の空間は戦時に避難所として機能するという役割を担ったのだった。

調査で訪れた2021年、私は残された地下防空壕の中に降りていった。

空気は湿っていたが、外からの光は床に届いていた。この地域の学童は福島県に集団疎開したという。東京大空襲に至る前にここに入ることなく逃げられたのだろうか。

何回かはここに身を潜めた親子もいたのだろうか。

内藤礼さんはまずその場を訪れ、しばらくたったある日、「ひと」をそこに遣わした。

時空を超えているそのひとは、大人たちの作った負の空間を見すえて立つ。

2021年の校庭では体育の授業に励む子供たちの声が響き、それは換気のために開けられた格子を通って地下の防空壕空間にも吸いこまれていく。そしてその様な循環が続くことを私たちは見届けなければと思う。平和の持続を見届けることの反面教師としての地下壕の存在ということも言える。

ひとは戦時の子供たちであり、現在の東京人であるという二面性を負って立っている。

もう戦争はしないでください、今ある戦争を許さない、という二つの祈りを込めてひとに立つことを私たちは託した。

Seeing things through

Kazuko Koike [Director in Chief, Tokyo Biennale 2021/2022]

As plans came together for a "local Tokyo-grown biennale," I opted for an air raid shelter under an elementary school in Taito Ward as an exhibition site. My prime motivation was thoughts of the fire-bombing that once engulfed the metropolis, even as wars still rage all over the world. The phrase "praying for Tokyo" came naturally to my lips. I told Rei Naito, an artist I dearly respect, and she responded immediately. Thereon began a tremulously unique spatial drama.

Let me first say a bit about myself. When artillery fire rained down on the Japanese archipelago during World War II, I was a third-year student in "National School" (the wartime name for elementary schools.) I had fled Tokyo to my step-parent's village of Kannami in Shizuoka Prefecture. It was an individual evacuation, as the government had ordered city children to be sent away to their relatives or whomever might look after them out in the countryside.

My stepfather ran a so-called youth training camp for young people from countries Japan had invaded were boarded while farming and raising cotton. Plants floursheds and fruit ripened in the mild Shizuoka climate, lush green *seri* ,or Japanese cress, grew wild down by a babbling brook. Most days I'd go sit on the banks, dip my feet in the swirling current, and sing nursery rhymes with my classmates. Never military anthems. It was a kind of paradise.

Even up in the hills they recommended air raid shelters, so my stepfather dug a small trench-cave in a nearby slope. Maybe it was in that shelter I overheard adults talking how the B29s that attacked Tokyo dropped their leftover bombs everywhere from the Izu Peninsula to Numazu Bay. I also recall the wartime routine of having to be on constant alert in case of a sudden incursion of enemy planes and getting upset with my grandmother during a meal in a tunnel. Whatever, at least I was with family. I have no idea how other kids who were evacuated collectively to unknown faraway places dealt with their lot.

Meanwhile, the government had pursued a program of building group shelters in city schools. And so the prospect of Rei Naito's participation in Tokyo Biennale 2021/2022 started with a survey of "surviving school ground bomb shelters." While here is not the place to discuss Japan's defeat and subsequent recovery, the fact is that practically all air raidshelters have disappeared without a trace from Tokyo. Even the notion of consecrating monuments to keep alive memories of the war and its horrors is fading over time. However, thanks to careful investigations on the part of the Tokyo Biennale Secretariat, we learned that a wartime shelter still existed under Kuromon Elementary School in Taito Ward.

And so it was, our vision of "praying for Tokyo" led us to Kuramae and the private gallery of Akiyoshi Taniguchi, photographer and resident priest of Chohouin temple, where architect Makoto Yokomizo had installed a distinctive minimalist exhibition space selected for its particular slant of external illumination. Therein, Rei Naito erected one of her works entitled *human*.

human is a wooden form born of the silence in the wake of 2011 Tohoku Earthquake-Tsunami. It is perhaps the smallest wooden sculpture imaginable. A faint shaft of light into that enclosed space barely reveals the presence of the tiny figure.
The priest then conducts us a minute's walk away from Chohouin to a wooden gate facing onto an ordinary neighborhood path and behind it a graveyard. There in one corner stands a statue of the Bodhisattva Jizo dedicated to the spirits of children whose lives were cut short in the firebombing of Tokyo. Naito sets a glass jar before Jizo and pours in water.

Many were those lost amidst the fires of war who wanted for water that day, many of them children. Names of girls and boys who perished are carved in the stone base of the statue. The glass jar placed before it is nothing special, just a typical lidded shape. Visitors to this Biennale exhibition site are asked to replenish water for the murdered children as it evaporates in the hot summer sun.

The bunker beneath Kuromon Elementary School completes the spatial configuration together with Rei Naito's Chohouin installation and the graveside prayer.

While the public school built after the 1923 Tokyo Earthquake in Ueno Kuromo-cho not far from the shopping street now bustling with tourists from abroad is recognized as an exemplary tremor-resistant structure, who knew that its basement served as an emergency refuge during the war? We went down to take a look as part of the 2021 search for surviving air raid shelters.

The air was damp, but daylight reached all the way to the floor. Schoolchildren from around here were said to have been evacuated en masse to Fukushima prefecture. Had they managed to escape without ever hiding here before the firebombing of Tokyo in March 1945.

First thing, Rei Naito visited the space, then a few days later she bequeathed [another] *human* here. That work now stands watch, transcending time and space, in the negative space hollowed out by adults.

In 2021 the voices of children exerting themselves at physical education in the schoolyard travels down through a ventilation grille to breathe life into the basement air raid shelter. We have to make sure that the air keeps circulating, just as the air raid shelter has to make sure by way of negative example that peace prevails.

human bears a dual identity, addressing both children in wartime and Tokyo dwellers today. We are the entrusted guardians of a two-fold prayer to never fight another war and never accept the wars of today.

展覧会:内藤礼「わたしは生きた」
東京ビエンナーレ2020/2021「東京に祈る」
キュレーション:小池一子(東京ビエンナーレ2020/2021 総合ディレクター)
主催:一般社団法人東京ビエンナーレ

会期:2021年7月17日[土]—9月5日[日]

作品・会場

pp. 23–27
《ひと》2012年/木にアクリル絵具/15×10×50 mm(長応院蔵)

会場:空蓮房(東京都台東区蔵前4-17-14 長応院内)
慶長7年(1602年)に創建された浄土宗の寺院・長応院内に、平成18年(2006年)9月11日に建立された瞑想ギャラリー。写真家でもある23世住職・谷口昌良によってつくられた空間では、2012年に内藤礼の展覧会「地上はどんなところだったか」も開催している。

pp. 05–07, 28
《無題》2021年/水、ガラス瓶/93×Φ70 mm

会場:長応院墓地(東京都台東区蔵前4-11-15)
昭和20年(1945年)3月9日夜から10日未明にかけて、アメリカ空軍のB29型爆撃機が東京の下町を中心に焼夷弾を投下した「東京大空襲」。親子地蔵尊は、その慰霊碑として昭和30年(1955年)3月10日に、町会によって長応院の墓地の一角に建立された。現在でも3月10日には慰霊法要がある。

pp. 10–19
《ひと》2021年/木にアクリル絵具/15×10×65 mm

会場:台東区立黒門小学校防空壕(非公開)
明治43年(1910年)5月7日に創立され、現役の学校として現在も児童たちが通う黒門小学校。校舎の地下にある防空壕は、今もそのまま残されている。関東大震災後の昭和5年(1930年)、復興小学校として当時最先端の防災対策が施された。

Exhibiton: Rei Naito "I have lived"
Tokyo Biennale 2020/2021 "Praying for Tokyo"
Curated by Kazuko Koike (Director in Chief, Tokyo Biennale 2020/2021)
Organized by General Non-Profit Incorporated Organization Tokyo Biennale

Dates: Saturday 17 July – Sunday 5 September 2021

Works and Venues

pp. 23–27
human 2012 / acrylic on wood / 15×10×50 mm (Collection of Chohouin Buddhist Temple)

Venue: Kurenboh Chohouin Buddhist Temple Gallery
(4-17-14 Kuramae, Taito-ku, Tokyo, Japan)
Kurenboh was inaugurated as a meditation gallery on 11 September 2006 at Chohouin, a Jodo Buddhist temple founded in 1602. The space was created by Akiyoshi Taniguchi, the 23rd head priest, who is also a photographer. Rei Naito's exhibition "What Kind of Place was the Earth?" was held at the gallery in 2012.

pp. 05–07, 28
untitled 2021 / water, glass jar / 93×Φ70 mm

Venue: Chohouin Buddhist Temple Cemetery (4-11-15 Kuramae, Taito-ku, Tokyo, Japan)
From the night of 9 March to the early morning of 10 March 1945, the Bombing of Tokyo took place when the U.S. Air Force B-29 bombers dropped incendiary bombs mainly on the Shitamachi [traditional shopping, entertainment, and residential district] of Tokyo. The Oyako Jizoson [parent and child Jizo Bodhisattva statue] was erected in a corner of the Chohouin Buddhist Temple Cemetery on 10 March 1955 by the neighborhood association as a memorial to the victims. A memorial service is still held every year on 10 March.

pp. 10–19
human 2021 / acrylic on wood / 15×10×65 mm

Venue: Taito Ward Kuromon Elementary School Air Raid Shelter (Not open to the public)
The Kuromon Elementary School, founded on 7 May 1910, is still attended by children today. The air raid shelter in the basement of the school building still exists. In 1930, after the Great Kanto Earthquake, the school was rebuilt and equipped with the most advanced disaster prevention measures of the time.

内藤礼

1961年広島生まれ。美術家。主な個展に「地上にひとつの場所を」佐賀町エキジビット・スペース（東京、1991年）、「地上にひとつの場所を」第47回ヴェネチア・ビエンナーレ日本館（1997年）、「Being Called」カルメル会修道院（フランクフルト、企画：フランクフルト近代美術館、1997年）、「すべて動物は、世界の内にちょうど水の中に水があるように存在している」神奈川県立近代美術館 鎌倉（2009年）、「信の感情」東京都庭園美術館（2014年）、「信の感情」パリ日本文化会館（2017年）、「Two Lives」テルアビブ美術館（2017年）、「明るい地上には あなたの姿が見える」水戸芸術館現代美術ギャラリー（2018年）、「うつしあう創造」金沢21世紀美術館（2020年）、「breath」ミュンヘン州立版画素描館（2023年）。パーマネント作品に、「このことを」家プロジェクト きんざ、直島（香川、2001年）、「母型」豊島美術館（香川、2010年）。

2011年《ひと》の制作を開始

《ひと》展示歴

個展

2011年　「佐賀町アーカイブCOLLECTION plus,2 内藤礼展」佐賀町アーカイブ、東京
2012年　「地上はどんなところだったか」ローク・ガレリー、ベルリン
　　　　「地上はどんなところだったか」ギャラリー小柳、東京
　　　　「地上はどんなところだったか」空蓮房、東京
　　　　「地上はどんなところだったか」奥共同店、沖縄
2014年　「信の感情」東京都庭園美術館、東京
2015年　「よろこびのほうが大きかったです」ギャラリー小柳、東京
2016年　「内藤礼」 丗 | SEI、京都
　　　　「color beginning」ローク・ガレリー、ベルリン
2017年　「信の感情」パリ日本文化会館、パリ
　　　　「Two Lives」テルアビブ美術館、テルアビブ
2018年　「明るい地上には あなたの姿が見える」水戸芸術館現代美術ギャラリー、茨城
2020年　「うつしあう創造」金沢21世紀美術館、石川

グループ展

2011年　「Masked Portrait Part II : When Vibrations Become Forms」
　　　　マリアン・ボエスキー・ギャラリー、ニューヨーク
2013年　「椿会2013―初心―」資生堂ギャラリー、東京
　　　　「アート・アーチ・ひろしま2013 ピース・ミーツ・アート!」広島県立美術館、広島
　　　　「反重力　浮遊｜時空旅行」豊田市美術館、愛知
2014年　「タマ/アニマ(わたしに息を吹きかけてください)内藤礼　畠山直哉 写真」ギャラリー小柳、東京
　　　　「椿会展2014―初心―」資生堂ギャラリー、東京
2015年　「椿会展2015―初心―」資生堂ギャラリー、東京
2016年　「椿会展2016―初心―」資生堂ギャラリー、東京
2017年　「椿会展2017―初心―」資生堂ギャラリー、東京
2018年　「Primal Water: An Exhibition of Japanese Contemporary Art」
　　　　ベラッジョ・ギャラリー・オブ・ファイン・アート、ラスベガス
2019年　「2019年度　第2期コレクション展」愛知県立美術館、愛知
2021年　「わたしは生きた」空蓮房、長応院墓地、台東区立黒門小学校防空壕
　　　　(東京ビエンナーレ2020/2021)、東京

パブリックコレクション

愛知県立美術館、愛知
イスラエル美術館、エルサレム
金沢21世紀美術館、石川
株式会社 資生堂、東京

Rei Naito

Born in 1961 in Hiroshima. Artist. Notable solo exhibitions include "une place sur la Terre" Sagacho Exhibit Space, Tokyo (1991), "une place sur la Terre" The Japan Pavilion, The 47th Venice Biennale, Venice (1997), "Being Called", Karmeliterkloster (Curation by Museum für Moderne Kunst, Frankfurt am Main, Germany)(1997), "Tout animal est dans le monde comme de l'eau à l'intérieur de l'eau." The Museum of Modern Art, Kamakura, Kanagawa (2009), "the emotion of belief" Tokyo Metropolitan Teien Art Museum, Tokyo (2014), " the emotion of belief" Maison de la Culture du Japon à Paris, Paris (2017), "Two Lives" Tel Aviv Museum of Art, Tel Aviv (2017), " on this bright Earth I see you" Contemporary Art Gallery, Art Tower Mito, Ibaraki (2018), " Mirror Creation" 21st Century Museum of Contemporary Art, Kanazawa, Ishikawa (2020), and "breath" Staatliche Graphosche Sammlung München, Munich (2023). Permanent installations include "Being given" (Kinza, Art House Project, Naoshima, Kagawa, 2001), "Matrix" (Teshima Art Museum, Teshima, Kagawa, 2010).

Rei Naito began making *human* in 2011.

Exhibition history of *human*

Solo Exhibitions

2011 "Sagacho Archives Collection plus, 2 –Rei Naito" Sagacho Archives, Tokyo, Japan
2012 "What Kind of Place was the Earth?" Loock Galerie, Berlin, Germany
"What Kind of Place was the Earth?" Gallery Koyanagi, Tokyo, Japan
"What Kind of Place was the Earth?" Kurenboh Chohouin Buddhist Temple Gallery, Tokyo, Japan
"What Kind of Place was the Earth?" Oku-kyodoten, Okinawa, Japan
2014 "the emotion of belief" Tokyo Metropolitan Teien Art Museum, Tokyo, Japan
2015 "The joys were greater" Gallery Koyanagi, Tokyo, Japan
2016 "Rei Naito" SEI, Kyoto, Japan
"color beginning" Loock Galerie, Berlin, Germany
2017 "the emotion of belief" Maison de la Culture du Japon à Paris, Paris, France
"Two Lives" Tel Aviv Museum of Art, Tel Aviv, Israel
2018 "on this bright Earth I see you"
Contemporary Art Gallery, Art Tower Mito, Ibaraki, Japan
2020 "Mirror Creation" 21st Century Museum of Contemporary Art, Kanazawa, Ishikawa, Japan

Group Exhibitions

2011 "Masked Portrait Part II: When Vibrations Become Forms"
Marianne Boesky Gallery, New York, USA
2013 "Tsubaki-kai 2013—Shoshin (beginnier's mind)" Shiseido Gallery, Tokyo, Japan
"Art Arch Hiroshima 2013: Peace Meets Art!"
Hiroshima Prefectural Art Museum, Hiroshima, Japan
"Antigravity" Toyota Municipal Museum of Art, Aichi, Japan
2014 "tama / anima (please breathe life into me) Rei Naito | photographs Naoya Hatakeyama"
Gallery Koyanagi, Tokyo, Japan
"Tsubaki-kai 2014—Shoshin (beginnier's mind)" Shiseido Gallery, Tokyo, Japan
2015 "Tsubaki-kai 2015—Shoshin (beginnier's mind)" Shiseido Gallery, Tokyo, Japan
2016 "Tsubaki-kai 2016—Shoshin (beginnier's mind)" Shiseido Gallery, Tokyo, Japan
2017 "Tsubaki-kai 2017—Shoshin (beginnier's mind)" Shiseido Gallery, Tokyo, Japan
2018 "Primal Water: An Exhibition of Japanese Contemporary Art"
Bellagio Gallery of Fine Art, Las Vegas, USA
2019 "From the Museum Collection 2019: Second Period"
Aichi Prefectural Museum of Art, Aichi, Japan
2021 "I have lived" Kurenboh Chohouin Buddhist Temple Gallery /
Chohouin Buddhist Temple Cemetery / Taito Ward Kuromon Elementary School Air Raid Shelter
(Tokyo Biennale 2020/2021), Tokyo

Public Collections

Aichi Prefectural Museum of Art, Aichi, Japan
The Israel Museum, Jerusalem, Israel
Shiseido Co., Ltd., Tokyo, Japan
21st Century Museum of Contemporary Art, Kanazawa, Ishikawa, Japan

内藤礼 わたしは生きた

発行日：2024年6月20日 第1刷

執筆
内藤礼
小池一子
写真
畠山直哉
デザイン
木村稔将
翻訳
管啓次郎（p.34）
アルフレッド・バーンバウム（pp.39–41）
柿沼ボニー（p.43）
協力
岡本夏佳（タカ・イシイギャラリー）
谷口昌良（空蓮房）
台東区立黒門小学校

発行者
中村水絵
〒154-0024
東京都世田谷区三軒茶屋2-48-3
三軒茶屋スカイハイツ708
Tel: 03-6824-6566
info@hehepress.com
www.hehepress.com

印刷・製本所
株式会社八紘美術

Printed in Japan
ISBN978-4-908062-59-9 C0070

Rei Naito: I have lived

First published in Japan, June 2024

Texts by
Rei Naito
Kazuko Koike
Photographs by
Naoya Hatakeyama
Design by
Toshimasa Kimura
Translated by
Keijiro Suga (p.34)
Alfred Birnbaum (pp. 39–41)
Bonnie Kakinuma (p.43)
Cooperation with
Natsuka Okamoto (Taka Ishii Gallery)
Akiyoshi Taniguchi (Kurenboh)
Taito Ward Kuromon Elementary School

Published by
Mizue Nakamura
HeHe
2-48-3 #708 Sangenjaya, Setagaya-ku, Tokyo
154-0024 Japan
Tel: +81(0)3-6824-6566
info@hehepress.com
www.hehepress.com

Printed and bound in Japan by
Hakkou Bijyutsu Co., Ltd.

ISBN978-4-908062-59-9 C0070